WORLD'S FAVORITE MUSIC FOR THE RECORDER

ARRANGED BY

ALEXANDER SHEALY

FOREWORD

The Recorder is the most popular of the pre-band melody instruments. Its popularity has been increasing year after year. It has proved itself a valuable introduction to eventual band training and solo work on band instruments.

This book contains 200 melodies, covering every class of music, from popular songs, folk songs, hymns and spirituals, dance tunes, to concert pieces. 30 selections have been arranged for duet and trio ensemble playing, and these may also be used

sively presented, lying principles ll guide the beginner from the very easiest stages all the way to pieces requiring a fair amount of technical ingenuity and musicianship. Lyrics and chord symbols (for accompanying instruments) are included in a majority of the selections.

We present this book in the hope that it will stimulate interest in music, develop hidden musical talent, and furnish many hours of entertainment and enjoyment.

The Publisher

ASHLEY PUBLICATIONS

EXCLUSIVELY DISTRIBUTED BY HAL•LEONARD®

CONTENTS

Printed in Canada

Fingering Charts

DO NOT CROSS BRIDGES BEFORE YOU COME TO THEM!
Use these charts only in conjunction with appropriate sections of this book.

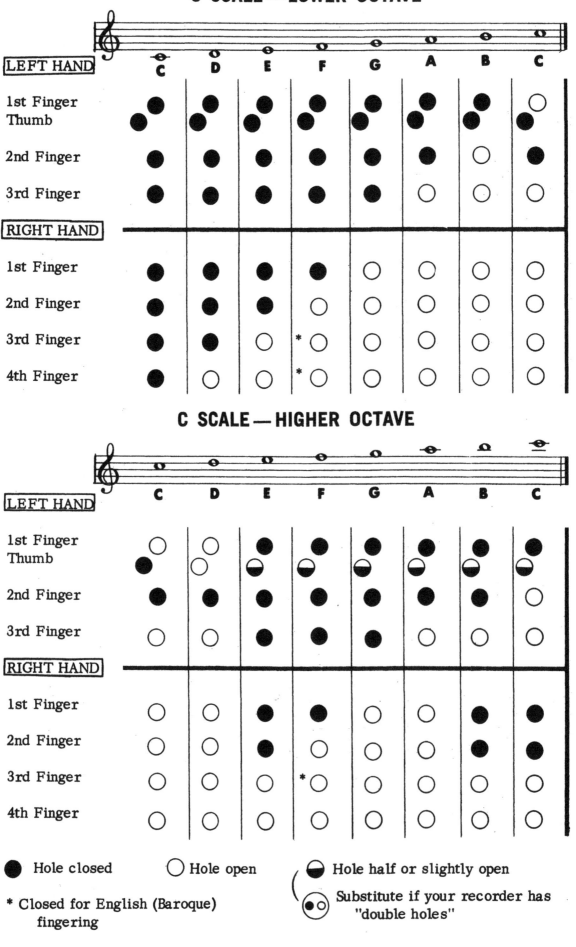

C SCALE — LOWER OCTAVE

C SCALE — HIGHER OCTAVE

● Hole closed   ○ Hole open   ◐ Hole half or slightly open

* Closed for English (Baroque) fingering   ⊙○ Substitute if your recorder has "double holes"

SHARPS AND FLATS — LOWER OCTAVE

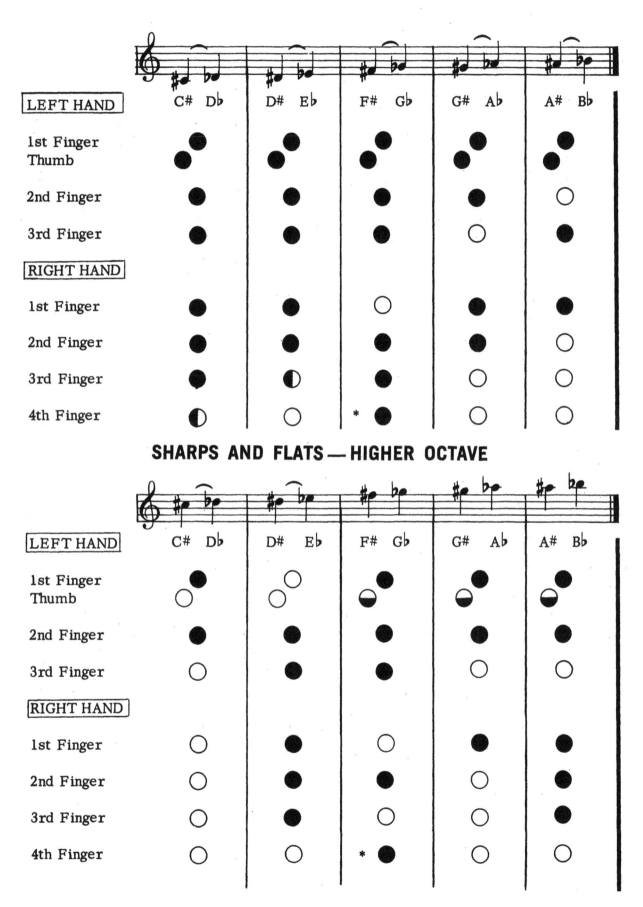

SHARPS AND FLATS — HIGHER OCTAVE

* OPEN for English (Baroque) Fingering

ELEMENTARY MUSIC PRINCIPLES

THE STAFF.   All music notes are placed on a STAFF-through the lines or in the spaces
between the lines.   The bottom line is referred to as Line 1, the bottom space -space
1.

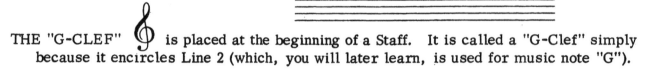

THE "G-CLEF" 𝄞 is placed at the beginning of a Staff.   It is called a "G-Clef" simply
because it encircles Line 2 (which, you will later learn, is used for music note "G").

MUSIC NOTES.   In paragraph "Timing", you will note various kinds of music notes.   In
the illustrations below, we show "whole notes".

NOTES ON LINES: E G B D F   IN SPACES: F A C E

Memory aid: Every good boy does   fine.

LINES AND SPACES: E F G A B C D E F

LEGER LINES AND SPACES.   These will show notes extending below and above the staff
(in alphabetic sequence):

C   D   G   A

BAR LINES.   These are vertical lines crossing the staff, as illustrated:

The space between two bar lines is a MEASURE, which divides music into equal Time
Units.   The double bar terminates a specific section of the piece and sometimes will
be found at the beginning of a piece.   A single bar plus a heavy bar indicates the con-
clusion of the piece.

TIMING (duration of the music notes).

Music is divided into "time units".   A "time signature" is indicated at the beginning
of a piece, like these: 2/4   3/4   6/8   4/4   * C

The TOP numbers show number of beats to a measure.   The BOTTOM numbers show
the "time value" of each beat, as follows:

WHOLE NOTE   o   4 beats

HALF NOTE   𝅗𝅥   2 beats

QUARTER NOTE   ♩   1 beat

* 4/4 and C are synonymous com-
mon time indicators. If C has a
vertical line through it: ¢ it means
"Cut Time", play faster.

EIGHTH NOTE ♪ or ♪ receives 1/2 beat.   It takes two 8th notes to give the same time duration as one quarter note.

Groups of 8th notes are usually printed with "beams", like this: ♫♫

We now show how time is counted.   Suppose the piece is in 4/4 time.   A WHOLE NOTE would fill the entire measure and receive the count of 1-2-3-4.   It would take two HALF NOTES to produce the same count.   The following illustrates the counting principle:

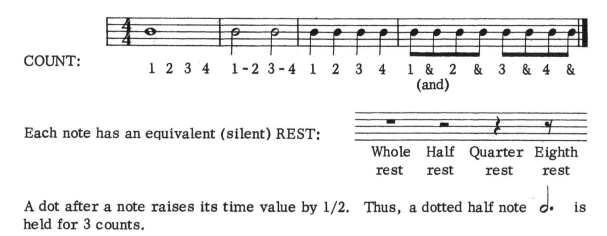

COUNT:

        1 2 3 4   1 - 2 3 - 4   1 2 3 4   1 & 2 & 3 & 4 &

                                        (and)

Each note has an equivalent (silent) REST:

                                    Whole Half Quarter Eighth
                                      rest   rest   rest   rest

A dot after a note raises its time value by 1/2.   Thus, a dotted half note ♩. is held for 3 counts.

TIES.   If two of the same notes are tied by a mark like this ‿ or ⌢ , hold the same note for the full time value of both.

ACCIDENTALS.   Occasions arise when notes must be altered in pitch. This is done by signs which are called "Accidentals", as follows:

♯   A "sharp" sign.   It raises the pitch of a note by 1/2 step.
♭   A "flat" sign.   It lowers the pitch of a note by 1/2 step.
♮   A "natural" sign.   It cancels a previous sharp or flat sign.

When an "accidental" is placed before a note, it is valid throughout the measure. For instance, if a sharp is placed before a C in a measure, any other C in that measure is raised 1/2 step unless it is cancelled by a natural sign.

KEY SIGNATURES.

A "key signature" is used in music to indicate the pitch of the notes - throughout the entire selection.   If there is no "key signature", it means that the piece is in the Key of C, without any sharps or flats, except as might arise as "accidentals". Otherwise, the key signature appears at the beginning of the staff, between the G Clef sign and the "time signature".   It consists of one or more sharps, or one or more flats.   These sharps or flats indicate that the notes which they represent are to be raised or lowered in pitch THROUGHOUT THE ENTIRE PIECE.

All F's are played as F# throughout the piece:

All B's are played as B♭ throughout the piece:

All B's and E's are played B♭ and E♭ throughout the piece:

REPEAT SIGN. A "Repeat Sign" is a pair of dots, one over the other like a colon, placed on the staff before or after a double bar, like this:

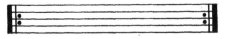

This indicates a section of the piece which is played and then repeated. If there's but one repeat sign (the 2nd in above illustration), it means repeat from the beginning of a piece or a specific section thereof. This is usually indicated by a sign ⅍ for example, DS ⅍ al Fine, means - Del Signo (from the Sign) to the designated end (Fine).

OCTAVES. An Octave is the distance from a lower tone to the same tone higher in pitch.

Sample octaves are illustrated:

Octave, low C to high C: Octave, low F to high F:

Octave, low D to high D: Octave, low G to high G:

STACCATO. You will sometimes see a light dot above or below a note. This means that the note is played "staccato", that is, lightly and crisply. (When the stem points up, the dot goes below the head of the note.)

PICK-UP NOTE(S).

You will occasionally see one or more notes before the opening measure of a selection which do not total the designated value of a full measure.

They are called "pick-up notes. The time needed to complete the value of a measure is compensated at the end of the piece, since every measure of the piece should have a specific number of beats.

For example, if there is a pick-up note in a measure of 4/4 time (and if it happens that it's a quarter note), you will only see 3 quarter notes at the end of the piece instead of 4 quarter notes, because you had to compensate for the pick-up note at the beginning.

CHORDS.

A "chord" is a harmonious combination of notes. We are here dealing with a melody instrument. The chord names above the melody lines, which you will find in much of the music in this book are used for accompaniment by piano, guitar, autoharp, etc.

DYNAMICS.

The suggestions for the speed and loudness of a piece are partially indicated:

Andante - "slow"		*pp*	"very soft"
Moderato - "moderate"		*p*	"soft"
Allegro - "fast"		*mf*	"moderately loud"
		f	"loud"

PLAYING THE RECORDER

The Recorder has 8 holes, 7 on front and 1 on back.   Fingering is as follows:

LEFT HAND: Hold Fingers 1-2-3 over the 3 holes nearest mouth-piece.
　　　　　　　The thumb (indicated by letter T) covers hole on back.

RIGHT HAND: Fingers 1-2-3-4 cover the remaining 4 holes.   The thumb
　　　　　　　is held under the instrument, thereby balancing it securely.

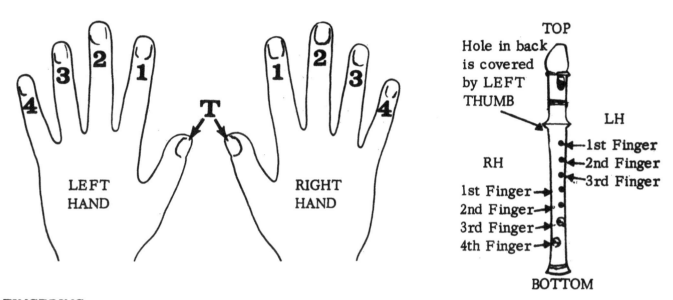

FINGERING:

The finger tips are not used, rather the soft pads of the fingers.   Cover the holes
firmly.   The left thumb covers the hole in back.   The instrument is supported by
the lips and the right thumb.   The thumb is positioned approximately behind first
finger of right hand.

The upper 3 holes utilize the first 3 fingers of the LEFT HAND; the lower 4 holes
utilize the 4 fingers of the RIGHT HAND.   The instrument is held at a 45° angle.

BREATHING AND BLOWING:

Blowing softly gives better tone quality.   Blow evenly. The harder, the sharper -
the softer, the lower the tone.

Take a quick breath (without losing the tempo) when you see a comma-like symbol
like this: ❜ A breath is taken at rests, double bars and repeat signs.

TONGUING:

The teeth and tongue do not touch the instrument.   The tongue has the natural ef-
fect of starting and stopping the tone.   The attack of the note is controlled by the
tongue.

To start a note, use the tongue and lightly pronounce "du". For crisp notes (like
"staccato"), use a quick "tu" instead of "du".   The "du" tonguing is for smoother
passages.

Before breath mark ❜ or at a rest, you stop the sound by placing tongue on the roof
of the mouth, thereby stopping the air flow.

Introducing G

MERRILY WE ROLL ALONG

FRENCH TUNE

HOT CROSS BUNS

Introducing High C

Count 1 2 3 4 1 2 3 4 1 2 3 4 1 2 3 4

Practice with A-B-C-G

Count 1 2 3 1 2 3 1 2 3 1 2 3 1 2 3 1 2 3 1 2 3

1 2 3 1 2 3 1 2 3 1 2 3 1 2 3 1 2 3 1 2 3 123 123

BARCAROLLE

Count 1 2 3 1 2 3 1 2 3 1 2 3 1 2 3 1 2 3 1 2 3 1 2 3

1 2 3 1 2 3 1 2 3 1 2 3 1 2 3 1 2 3 1 2 3 1 2 3

OLD ENGLISH AIR

Count 1 2 3 4 1 2 3 4 1 2 3 4 1 2 3 4 1 2 3 4 1 2 3 4 1 2 3 4

13

Introducing High D

Count 1 2 3 4 1 2 3 4 1 2 3 4 1234 1 2 3 1 2 3 1 2 3 1 2 3

THE CUCKOO

Count 3 1 2 3 1 2 3 1 2 3 1 2 3 1 2 3 1 2 3 1 2 3

1 2 3 1 2 3 1 2 3 1 2 3 1 2 3 1 2 3 1 2 3 1 2 3 1 2

(the 3rd count was in the "pick up")

SLEEP, BABY, SLEEP

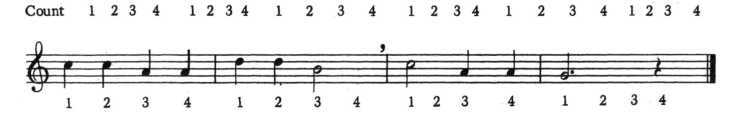

Count 1 2 3 4 1 2 3 4 1 2 3 4 1 2 3 4 1 2 3 4 1 2 3 4

1 2 3 4 1 2 3 4 1 2 3 4 1 2 3 4

AUNT RHODY

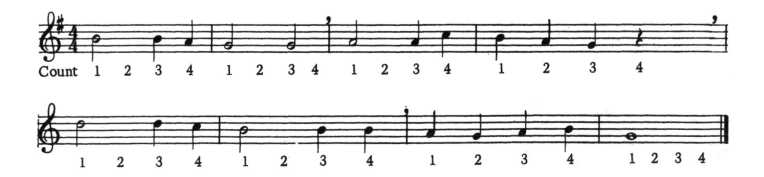

Count 1 2 3 4 1 2 3 4 1 2 3 4 1 2 3 4

1 2 3 4 1 2 3 4 1 2 3 4 1 2 3 4

We introduce here "Chord Names" above the melody lines.   These are for ACCOMPANIMENT only, by chorded instruments, such as Piano, Organ, Autoharp, &c.

JINGLE BELLS

WHEN THE SAINTS GO MARCHING IN

New Note-Low F

Count 1 2 3 4 1 2 3 4 1 2 3 4 1 2 and 3 4 and 1 2 3 4 1 2 3 4

GOING HOME

SHORTNIN' BREAD

New Note-Low E

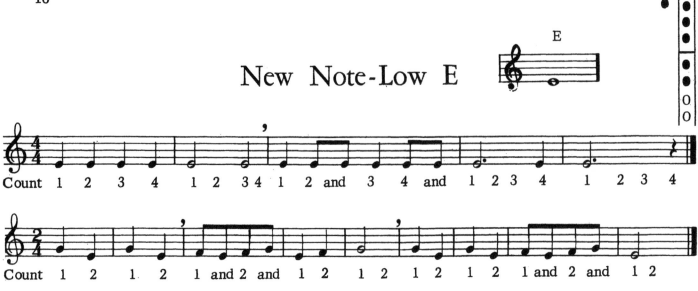

MARTHA

F. von Flotow

THE WAYFARING STRANGER

NOTE - Our "Time counting" will be discontinued from this point on.   You are "on your own".
(Reminder - Chord names are for accompanying instruments only.)

New Note-Low D

OLD MacDONALD

* Reminder:
C ¢ and 4/4 are similar time indicators. ¢ is played faster.

NOBODY KNOWS THE TROUBLE I'VE SEEN

GOOD-NIGHT, LADIES

New Note-Low C

C MAJOR SCALE (A scale is a series of tones forming the familiar "do re mi fa sol la ti do".)

C D E F G A B C C B A G F E D C

THIS OLD MAN

Brightly

REUBEN AND RACHEL

Moderately

HUSH, LITTLE BABY

Moderately

ON TOP OF OLD SMOKY

JULIDA POLKA

ROW, ROW, ROW YOUR BOAT

FRÈRE JACQUES

O SUSANNA

Stephen Foster

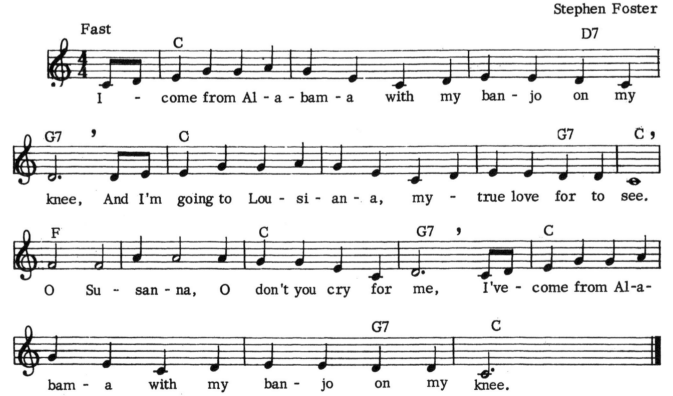

'ROUND HER NECK SHE WEARS A YELLOW RIBBON

Brightly

IT'S HARD, AIN'T IT HARD?

Rather slowly

It's Hard, Ain't It Hard, Ain't It Hard? To give love that won't come back to you. It's Hard, Ain't It Hard, Ain't It real real hard, To love you, my love, the way I do?

OLD BLACK JOE

LI'L LIZA JANE

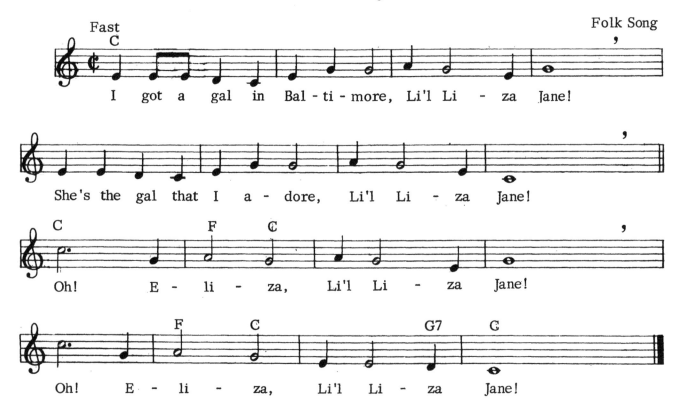

MICHAEL
(Row the Boat Ashore)

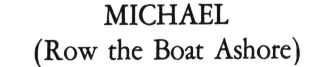

Moderately

Mi-chael, row the boat a-shore, Hal - le - lu - jah, Mi - chael,

row the boat a-shore, Hal - le - lu - jah!

AULD LANG SYNE

Moderately   Robert Burns

Should auld ac-quaint-ance be for - got and nev - er brought to

mind? Should auld ac-quaint-ance be for - got and - days of auld lang

syne? For auld - lang - syne, my friends, For auld - lang -

syne, We'll take a cup o' kind - ness yet, For - auld - lang - syne.

BUFFALO GALS

Fast

New Note-High E

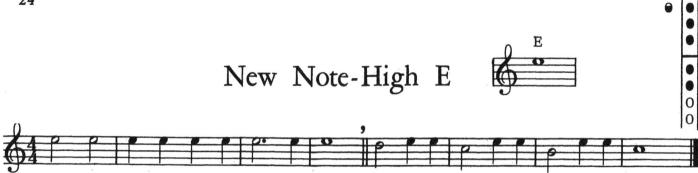

TWINKLE, TWINKLE, LITTLE STAR

IT CAME UPON A MIDNIGHT CLEAR

Sears - Willis

MY WILD IRISH ROSE

Chauncey Olcott

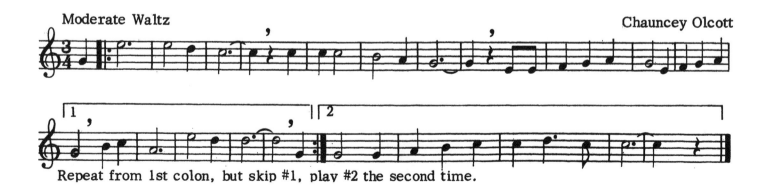

Repeat from 1st colon, but skip #1, play #2 the second time.

New Note-F#

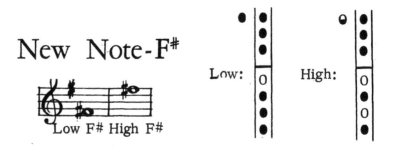

Low F# High F#

Music in the key of G is identified by a # sign on the upper F line, which affects every F in the piece, whether low F or high F.   All F's are played as F# unless cancelled by a 'natural"(♮) sign.   In "Daisy Bell" we shall show the # before each F just to get you used to it. Thereafter, don't forget the command of the key signature - F# in the signature, all F's are F#.)

A BICYCLE BUILT FOR TWO
(Daisy Bell)

HENRY DACRE

HAND ME DOWN MY WALKING CANE

FOLK SONG

New Note-High G

SCALE IN G MAJOR

THE SIDEWALKS OF NEW YORK

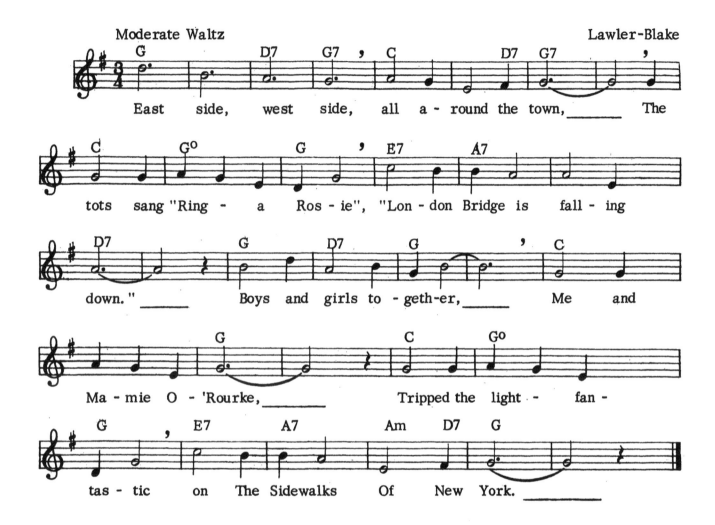

BIRTHDAY THEME

28

HAIL! HAIL! THE GANG'S ALL HERE!

MY DARLING CLEMENTINE

SKIP TO MY LOU

Brightly

Folk Dance

WE WISH YOU A MERRY CHRISTMAS

Bright waltz tempo

Christmas Song

We wish you a mer-ry Christmas, We wish you a merry Christmas, We

wish you a merry Christmas and a Hap-py New Year! Fine

DS al Fine

SWEET MOLLY MALONE

In Dub-lin's fair cit-y, Where girls are so pret-ty, 'Twas

there that I first saw sweet Mol-ly Ma-lone, She - drove a wheel-

bar-row, Thru streets broad and nar-row, Sing-ing "Cock-les and mus-sels, a-

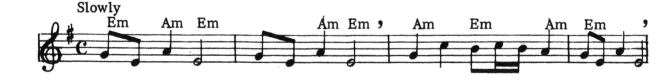

live a-live oh!" A - live, a-live oh ___, A - live a-live

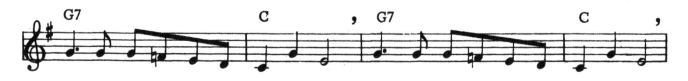

oh! ___ Sing-ing "Cock-les and mus-sels, a - live a - live oh!"

SONG OF THE VOLGA BOATMEN

CARRY ME BACK TO OLD VIRGINNY

DOWN IN THE VALLEY

Moderate waltz

Folk Song

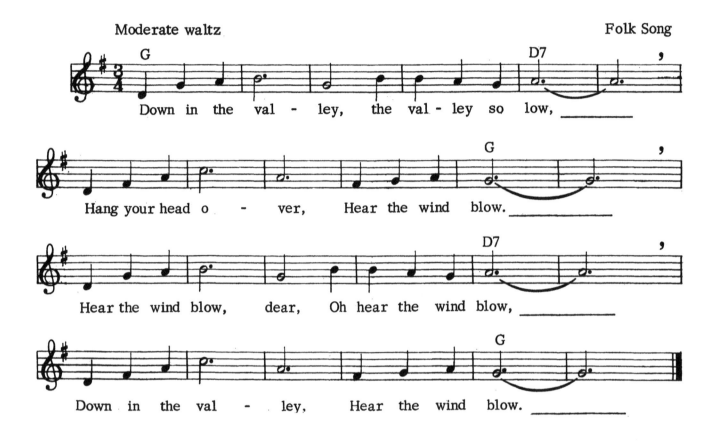

Down in the val - ley, the val - ley so low, _____

Hang your head o - ver, Hear the wind blow. _____

Hear the wind blow, dear, Oh hear the wind blow, _____

Down in the val - ley, Hear the wind blow. _____

GIVE ME THAT OLD TIME RELIGION

With spirit

Spiritual

Give me that old time re - li - gion, Give me that old time re -

li-gion, Give me that old time re - li - gion, It's good e-nough for me.

It was good for the He-brew chil-dren, it was good for the He-brew children, It was

good for the He-brew chil-dren, And it's good e - nough for me. _____

OH! THEM GOLDEN SLIPPERS

Brightly

James A. Bland

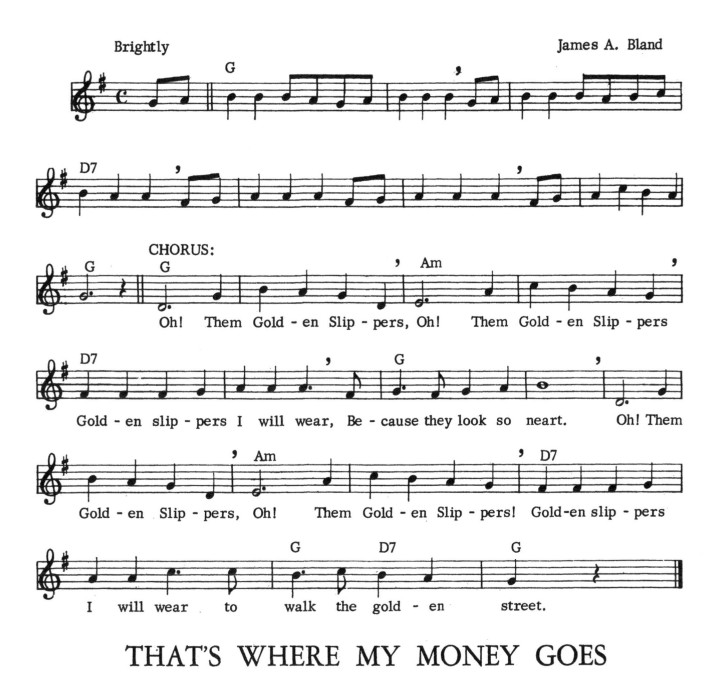

CHORUS:

Oh! Them Gold - en Slip - pers, Oh! Them Gold - en Slip - pers Gold - en slip - pers I will wear, Be - cause they look so neart. Oh! Them Gold - en Slip - pers, Oh! Them Gold - en Slip - pers! Gold-en slip - pers I will wear to walk the gold - en street.

THAT'S WHERE MY MONEY GOES

Rather fast

Folk Song

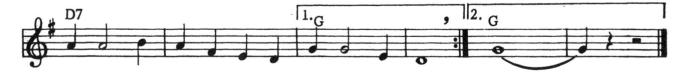

RED RIVER VALLEY

Moderately

Western Song

From this val - ley, they say, you are go - ing, ____ I will
So come sit here a - while ere you leave us, ____ Do not

miss your sweet face and your smile, Just be - cause you are wea - ry and
has - ten to bid us a - dieu, Just re - mem - ber the Red Riv - er

tir - ed, You are chang-ing your range for a while.
Val - ley, And the cow - boy who loves you so true.

HOME ON THE RANGE

Moderately

Western Song

Oh give me a home where the buf - fa - lo roam, Where the

deer and the an - te - lope play, ____ Where sel-dom is heard a dis-

cour-ag-ing word, And the skies are not cloud - y all day. ____

Home, home on the range, Where the deer and the an - te - lope play, ____

____ Where sel - dom is heard a dis - cour - ag - ing word, And the

skies are not cloud - y all day. ____

BLUE BELLS OF SCOTLAND

Moderately

Scottish Song

Oh where, oh - where - is your high-land lad - die gone? Oh
where, oh - where - is your high - land lad - die gone? He's
gone to fight the foe, For King - George up - on the throne, And it's
oh! in my heart, how I - wish him safe at home.

THE WABASH CANNONBALL

Folk Song

With spirit

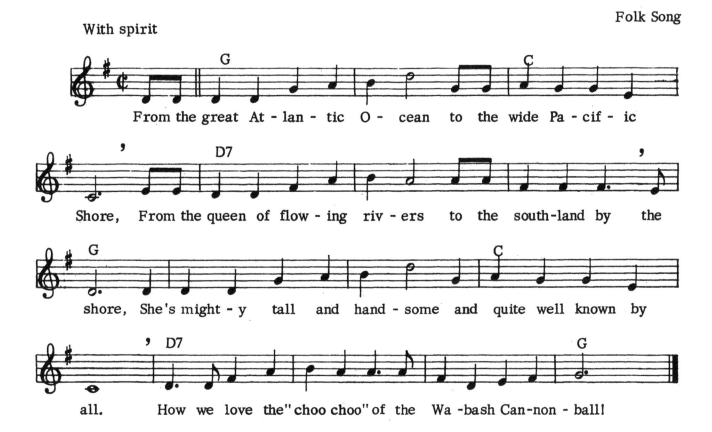

From the great At - lan - tic O - cean to the wide Pa - cif - ic
Shore, From the queen of flow - ing riv - ers to the south-land by the
shore, She's might - y tall and hand - some and quite well known by
all. How we love the "choo choo" of the Wa - bash Can - non - ball!

THERE IS A TAVERN IN THE TOWN

With spirit

Folk Song

There is a tav - ern in the town (in the town), And

there my true love sits him down, Sits him down - and -

drinks his wine mid laugh - ter gay and free, And

nev - er nev - er thinks of me. Fare thee well for I must leave thee, do not

let the part-ing grieve thee, And re - mem-ber that the best of friends must

part, must part, A - dieu, a - dieu, kind friends, a - dieu (a - dieu a - dieu), I

can no long - er stay with you (stay with you -) I will

hang my harp on a weep - ing wil - low tree, And

may the world go well with thee!

Introducing B♭

In the key of F (which you will easily identify from the scale in the first exercise below), all notes B are flatted to B♭. A flat (♭) lowers the pitch of a note by 1/2 tone. The key of F has one flat (B♭) and the key is identified by a ♭ on the middle line of the staff, after the clef sign. It affects every B in the piece, unless naturalized by natural sign.

To accustom you to playing B♭ instead of B, we have used ♭ signs in the tune "America". Thereafter, you will bear it in mind. Don't forget to flat your B's in the key of F!

SCALE OF F

(all B's above are B♭)

F G A B♭ C D E F

AMERICA

Moderately

F Bb C7 , F Bb F Dm , Bb F C7

My coun - try, 'tis of thee, Sweet land of li - ber - ty, Of thee I

F , , C7 ,

sing. Land where my fa - thers died, Land of the pil - grim's pride,

F , Bb F C7 F

From ev - 'ry - moun-tain-side, Let - free - dom ring.

THE MEXICAN HAND-CLAPPING SONG

IN THE GLOAMING

Moderately   Ored - Harrison

In the gloam-ing, Oh my dar - ling, when the lights are

dim and low, And the qui - et shad - ows fall - ing soft - ly

come and soft - ly go. Where the winds are sob - bing -

faint - ly, with a gen - tle un - known - woe, Will you think of

me and love me, As you did once long a - go.

LONG LONG AGO

Moderately   Thomas Bayly

Tell me the tales that to me were so dear, Long long a -

go, Long long a - go. Sing me the songs I de - light - ed to

hear, Long long a - go, long a - go! (Fine)

DS 𝄋 al Fine

ANDANTINO

Slowly

EDWIN LEMARE

ABIDE WITH ME

Slowly

Lyte-Monk

A - bide with me, Fast falls the e - ven - tide,

The dark - ness deep - ens, Lord, with me a - bide.

When oth - er help - ers fail and com - forts flee,

Help of the help - less, oh a - bide with me.

HE'S GOT THE WHOLE WORLD
IN HIS HANDS

SWING LOW, SWEET CHARIOT

WE THREE KINGS OF ORIENT ARE

AWAY IN A MANGER

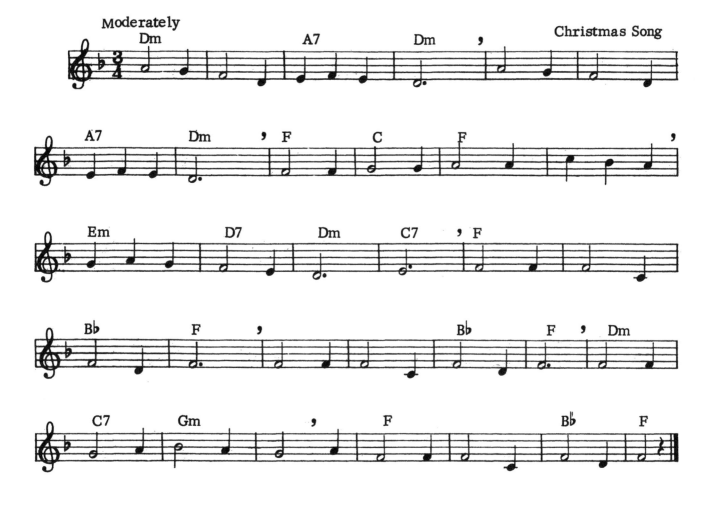

FLOW GENTLY, SWEET AFTON

Burns - Spilman

Flow gent-ly, sweet - Af - ton, a - mong thy green braes, Flow gent-ly, I'll sing thee a song in thy praise. My Mary's a - sleep by thy mur - mur - ing stream, Flow gent-ly, sweet Af - ton, dis - turb not her dream. Thou stock dove whose ech-o re - sounds from the hill, Ye — wild whistling blackbirds in yon - thorn - y - dell, Thou green crest-ed - lap wing, thy scream-ing fore-bear, I charge you, dis - turb not my slum-ber-ing fair.

FOR HE'S A JOLLY GOOD FELLOW

Spirited

SONG OF HAITI

Moderate calypso

LA CUCARACHA

Bright rumba tempo

LULLABY.

JOHANNES BRAHMS

Moderately

*1/16 notes (2 = 1 8th note)

LOVE'S OLD SWEET SONG

Words by
G. CLIFTON BINGHAM

Music by
JAMES L. MOLLOY

Slow

Once in the dear dead days be-yond re-call, When on the world the mists be-gan to fall,

Out of the dreams that rose in hap - py throng, Low to our hearts love sang an old sweet song,

And in the dusk where fell the fire-light's gleam, Soft-ly it wove it-self in - to our dream.

REFRAIN (somewhat faster)

Just a song at twi-light, When the lights are low, And the flick-'ring shad-ows

soft - ly come and go. Tho' the heart be wear-y, Sad the day and long,

Still to us at twi-light, Comes love's old song, Comes lov'es - old sweet - song.

I LOVE YOU TRULY

CARRIE JACOBS-BOND

I love you tru - ly, tru - ly dear,

Life with its sor - row, Life with its tear,

Fades in - to dreams when I feel you are near,

For I love you tru - ly, tru - ly dear.

FINLANDIA

JAN SIBELIUS

FIFTH SYMPHONY
(Theme)

PETER ILYICH TSCHAIKOWSKY

Slowly

The Key of D Major

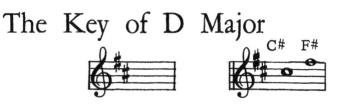

The key of D is identified by TWO SHARPS, on the F line and the C line. Both F and C become F# and C# throughout the piece.

This key introduces a new note, C#

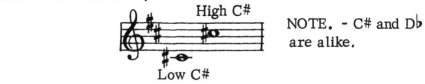

NOTE. - C# and D♭ are alike.

Practice a few measures with the new notes, as well as the scale in D major.

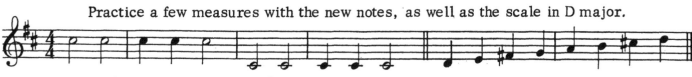

ALL C's, low or high, are C# in the above measures.

SWEET BETSY FROM PIKE

Moderate waltz   FOLK SONG

MELODY

NOTE. - This piece is in the key of G, which requires sharping only the F's. Therefore, the C#'s here are "accidentals". Note the "natural" in measure 5, restoring C to plain C.

Moderately   ANTON RUBINSTEIN

The Key of B♭ Major

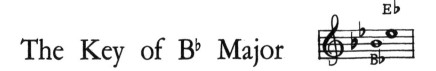

The key of B♭ Major is identified by 2 flats, on the B line and in the E space. Any B or E in the piece automatically becomes B♭ and E♭ without the necessity of a flat (♭) sign before the notes. This key introduces 4 new notes for your recorder:

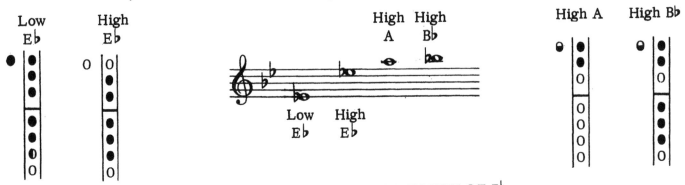

EXERCISES FOR ALL NEW NOTES — AND SCALE IN KEY OF B♭

GLORY, GLORY, HALLELUJAH

We continue, in this piece, to show the individual flat signs.

DRINK TO ME ONLY WITH THINE EYES

Now you're "on your own". Remember to flat each B and E (unless "naturalized" by sign).

HAVAH NAGILAH

Introducing High B
(also introduces C#)

SANTA LUCIA

The Key of A
(Which introduces new note, G#)

Music in the key of A is identified by 3 sharps, F# C# and G#.

EXERCISES and the "A" SCALE:

A B C# D E F# G# A

All G's, low or high, are sharped in the above.
All C's, F's and G's are sharped throughout a piece in the Key of A, unless "naturalized".

O COME ALL YE FAITHFUL
(ADESTE FIDELES)

A A E A B E C# B C# D C# B A A G# F#

G# A B C# G# F# E E E D C# D C# B C# A B

G# F# E A A G# A B A E C# C# B C# D

C# B C# D C# B A G# A D C# B A A

THREE BLIND MICE

NOTE. - In counting 6/8 time (six 8th notes to a measure), accent the 1st and 4th counts.

Count 1 2 3 1 2 3 1 2 3 4 5 6 1 2 3 1 2 3 1 2 3 4 5 6 1 2 3 1 2 3 1 2 3 4 5 6 1 2 3 4 5 6

C# B A C# B A E D D C# E D D

1 2 3 4 5 6 1 2 3 4 5 6 1 2 3 4 5 6 1 2 3 4 5 6

C# ___ E A A G# F# G# A E E E A A A G# F# G#

1 2 3 4 5 6 1 2 3 4 5 6 1 2 3 4 5 6 1 2 3 4 5 6 1 2 3 4 5 6

A E E E A A A G# F# G# A E E E D C# B A

BLUE DANUBE WALTZ

Top C

(Introducing Top C)

Moderate waltz

Johann Strauss

The Key of E♭

High E♭
Low E♭

LOW HIGH
E♭ E♭

The key of E♭ major is identified by 3 flat signs, B♭ E♭ and A♭.   All
are flatted throughout the piece, unless "naturalized" by the natural sign.

Similar tones and fingering: A# and B♭, D# and E♭, G# and A♭

EXERCISE:

THE SCALE IN E♭

E♭ F G A♭ B♭ C D E♭   E♭ D C B♭ A♭ G F E♭

MELODY IN E♭

Moderately

JOHANN SEBASTIAN BACH

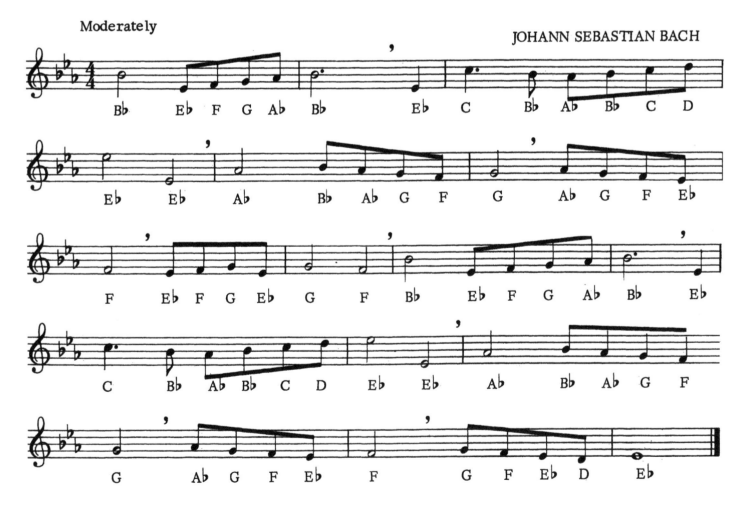

NOTE. - Refer to charts on Page 5 for fingering of A♭ (same as G#).

MASSA'S IN THE COLD COLD GROUND

STEPHEN FOSTER

BELIEVE ME, IF ALL THOSE ENDEARING YOUNG CHARMS

THOMAS MOORE

Be - lieve me, if all those en - dear-ing young charms, Which I

gaze on so fond - ly to - day, _____ Were to change by to -

mor-row and flee from my arms, Like - fair - y gifts fad - ing a - way, ___

___ Thou would still be a - dored, as this mo - ment thou art, Let thy love-li-ness fade as it

will, ___ And a - round the dear ru - in, each wish of my

heart would en - twine it - self ver - dant - ly still. ___

OVER THE WAVES

Moderate waltz

JUVENTINO ROSAS

GERMAN DANCE

Brightly

Folk Tune

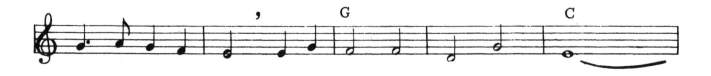

MOSCOW NIGHTS

V. Soloviev-Sedoy

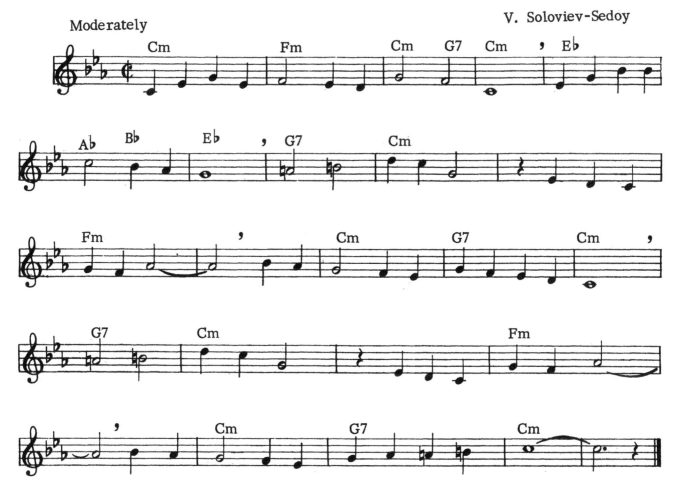

YOU'RE A GRAND OLD FLAG

With spirit (march tempo)

George M. Cohan

GOLD AND SILVER WALTZ

Moderate waltz

Franz Lehar

HATIKVOH

Rather slowly

Hebrew national anthem

AFTER THE BALL

Moderate waltz

Charles K. Harris

Af - ter the ball is o - ver, Af - ter the

break of morn, _____ Af - ter the danc - ers'

leav - ing, Af - ter the stars are gone. _____

Man - y a heart is ach - ing,

If you could read them all, _____

Man - y the hopes that have van - ished,

Af - ter the ball!

BEAUTIFUL BROWN EYES

Moderate waltz   Folk Song

Dar - ling, my dar - ling, I love you, _____

Love you with all my heart. _____ To -

mor - row we might have been mar - ried, _____ But

roam - ing has kept us a - part. _____

Beau - ti - ful, beau - ti - ful brown eyes, _____

Beau - ti - ful, beau - ti - ful brown eyes, Oh

beau - ti - ful, beau - ti - ful brown eyes, _____ I'll

nev - er love blue eyes a - gain. _____

ALOUETTE

Rather fast tempo

French folk tune

BEAUTIFUL ISLE OF SOMEWHERE

Slowly

Pounds - Fearis

Some-where the sun is shin - ing, Some-where the song-birds dwell. -

Hush then thy sad re - pin - ing, God lives! And all - is well.

Some - where, some - where, Beau - ti - ful Isle - of Some - where!

Land of the true where we live a - new, Beau-ti- ful Isle - of Somewhere!

I'VE BEEN WORKING ON THE RAILROAD

Moderately

Folk Song

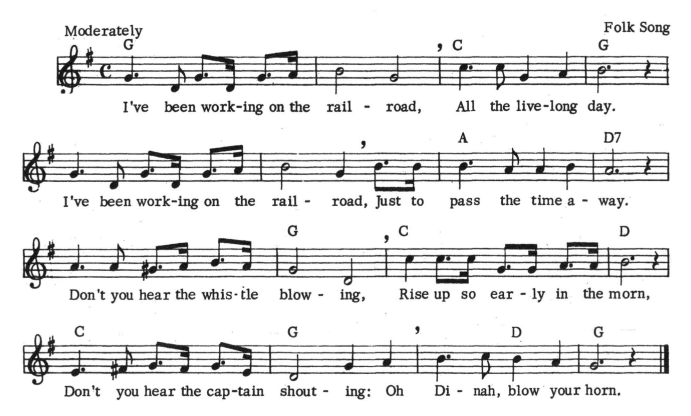

I've been work-ing on the rail - road, All the live-long day.

I've been work-ing on the rail - road, Just to pass the time a - way.

Don't you hear the whis-tle blow - ing, Rise up so ear - ly in the morn,

Don't you hear the cap-tain shout - ing: Oh Di - nah, blow your horn.

I GAVE MY LOVE A CHERRY

Moderately

Folk Song

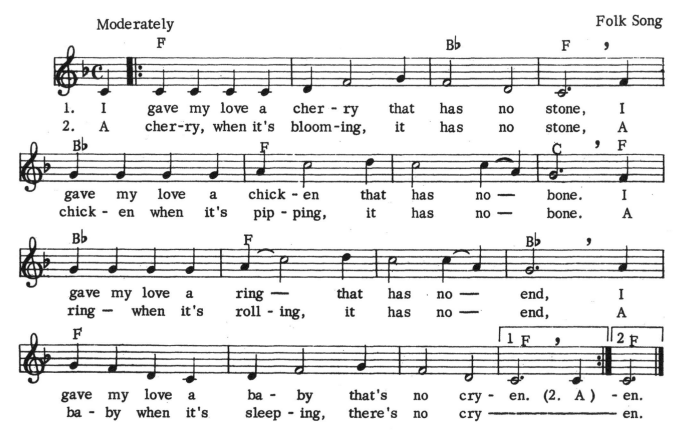

1. I gave my love a cher - ry that has no stone, I
2. A cher-ry, when it's bloom-ing, it has no stone, A

gave my love a chick - en that has no — bone. I
chick - en when it's pip - ping, it has no — bone. A

gave my love a ring — that has no — end, I
ring — when it's roll - ing, it has no — end, A

gave my love a ba - by that's no cry - en. (2. A) - en.
ba - by when it's sleep - ing, there's no cry ——————————— en.

62

HEAR THEM BELLS

O CHRISTMAS TREE

THE TWELVE DAYS OF CHRISTMAS

Moderately, with stepped-up tempo after 5th day

Christmas Song

6th - 12th days:
6 geese a-laying (repeat 5 to 1)
7 swans a-swimming (repeat 6 to 1)
8 maids a-milking (repeat 7 to 1)
9 ladies dancing (repeat 8 to 1)

10 lords a-leaping (repeat 9 to 1)
11 pipers piping (repeat 10 to 1)
12 drummers drumming
   (repeat 11 to 1)

LITTLE BUTTERCUP

Moderate waltz tempo

GILBERT & SULLIVAN

IN THE GOOD OLD SUMMER TIME

Moderate waltz

Shields - Evans

In the good old Sum - mer - time, _____ In the good old Sum - mer - time. _____ Stroll - ing through the shad - y lanes with your "ba - by mine". _____ You hold her hand and she holds yours, And that's a ver - y good sign _____ That she's your toot - sie woot - sie in the good old Sum - mer-time. _____

DOWN BY THE STATION

Brightly

Folk Song

Down by the sta - tion, Ear - ly in the morn - ing, See the lit - tle puf - fer - bel - lies all in a row. See the en - gine mas - ter turn a lit - tle han-dle, Choo choo, puff puff, Off they go!

LITTLE ANNIE ROONEY

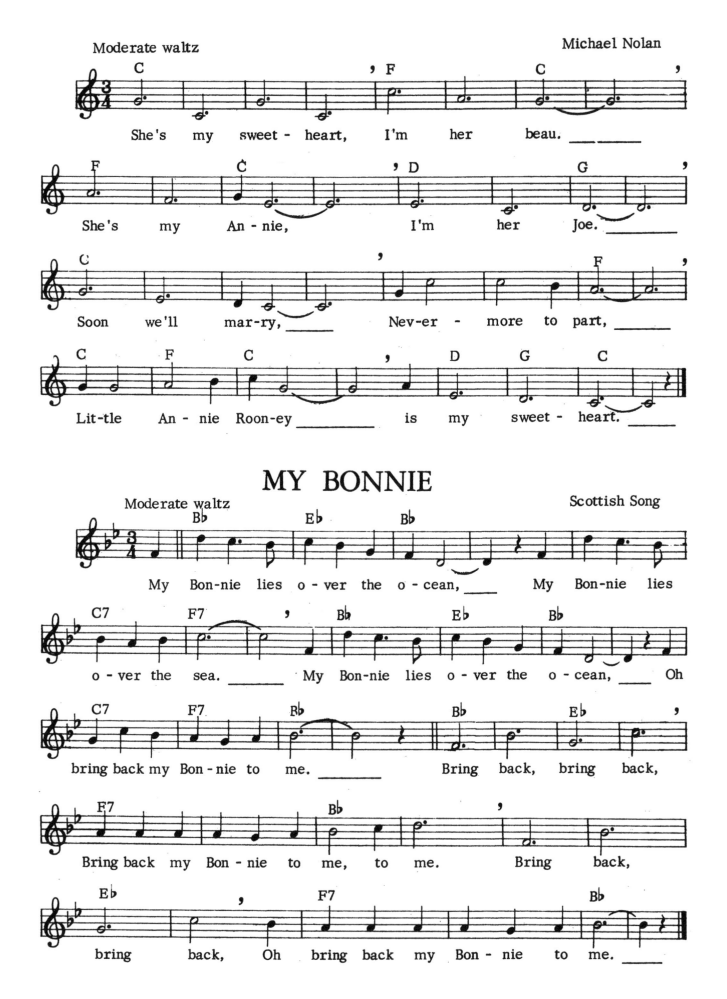

Moderate waltz

Michael Nolan

She's my sweet - heart, I'm her beau. _____ _____

She's my An - nie, I'm her Joe. _____

Soon we'll mar-ry, _____ Nev-er - more to part, _____

Lit-tle An - nie Roon-ey _____ is my sweet - heart. _____

MY BONNIE

Moderate waltz

Scottish Song

My Bon-nie lies o - ver the o - cean, _____ My Bon-nie lies

o - ver the sea. _____ My Bon-nie lies o - ver the o - cean, _____ Oh

bring back my Bon - nie to me. _____ Bring back, bring back,

Bring back my Bon - nie to me, to me. Bring back,

bring back, Oh bring back my Bon - nie to me. _____

RAISINS AND ALMONDS

Slowly

Yiddish Melody

POLLY WOLLY DOODLE

Brightly

Folk Song

Oh I went down South for to see my Sal, sing-ing "Pol-ly Wol-ly Doo-dle" all the day. Oh my dear sweet Sal is a live-ly gal, Sings "Pol-ly Wol-ly Doo-dle" all the day.

Fare thee well, Fare thee well, Fare thee well, my fai-ry fay, For I'm

gwine to Lou-si-an-na, my gui-tar and her "pi-a-na", ___ Sing-ing

"Pol-ly Wol-ly Doo-dle" all the day, Sing-ing "Pol-ly Wol-ly Doo-dle" all the day.

THE CAMPTOWN RACES

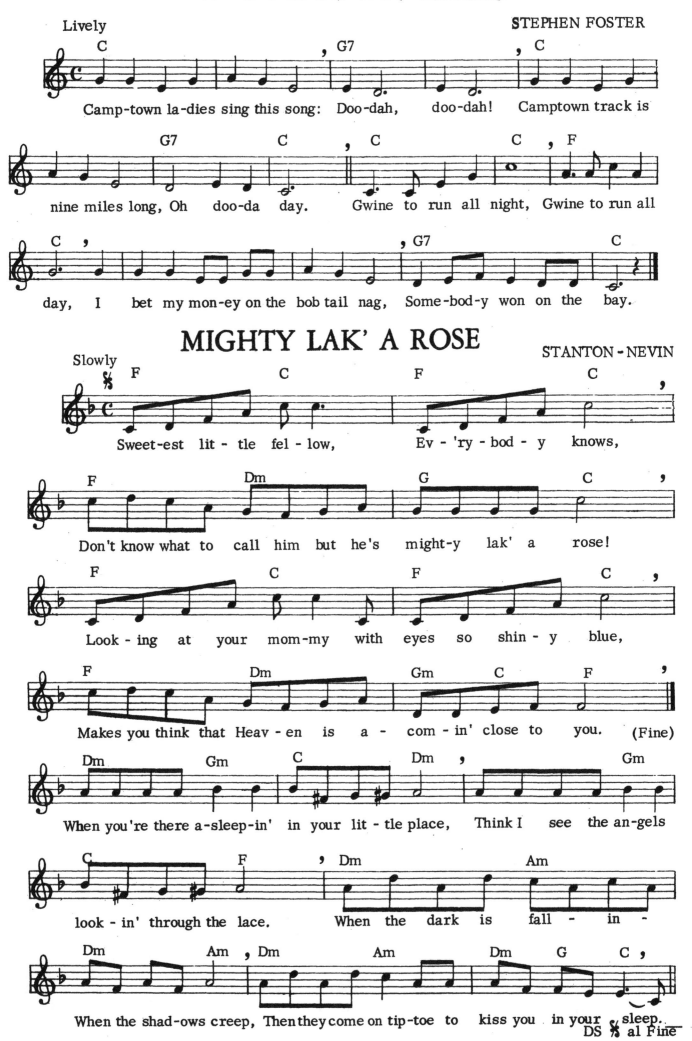

MIGHTY LAK' A ROSE

THE GLOW WORM

Moderately (gavotte)

PAUL LINCKE

HELENA POLKA

Bright polka tempo

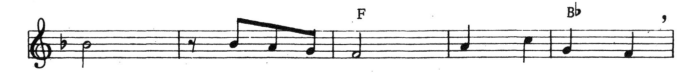

BILL BAILEY
(Won't You Please Come Home?)

Moderately

HUGHIE CANNON

Won't you come home, Bill Bai - ley, won't you come home?

She moans the whole day long.___ I'll do the cook-ing, hon-ey,

I'll pay the rent, I know I've done you wrong._____

Mem-ber the rain - y eve - ning I threw you out, With noth-in' but a

fine tooth comb?_____ I know I'm to blame, well ain't that a

shame? Bill Bai - ley, won't you please come home? _____

GYPSY LOVE SONG

Words by
HARRY SMITH

Music by
VICTOR HERBERT

WHISPERING HOPE

Moderately

ALICE HAWTHORNE

NEARER, MY GOD, TO THEE

WERE YOU THERE?

KUM-BA-YAH

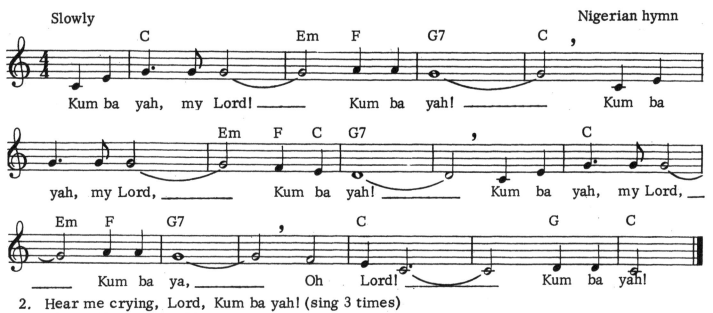

Slowly   Nigerian hymn

Kum ba yah, my Lord! _____ Kum ba yah! _____ Kum ba

yah, my Lord, _____ Kum ba yah! _____ Kum ba yah, my Lord, ___

_____ Kum ba ya, _____ Oh Lord! _____ Kum ba yah!

2. Hear me crying, Lord, Kum ba yah! (sing 3 times)
Oh Lord! Kum ba yah!

3. Hear me praying, Lord, Kum ba yah! (sing 3 times)
Oh Lord! Kum ba yah!

4. Oh I need you, Lord, Kum ba yah! (sing 3 times)
Oh Lord! Kum ba yah!

THE CRUEL WAR IS RAGING

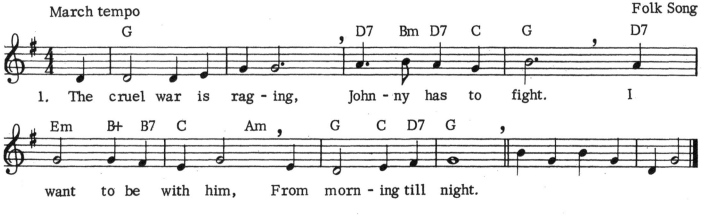

March tempo   Folk Song

1. The cruel war is rag - ing, John - ny has to fight. I

want to be with him, From morn - ing till night.

2. Oh Johnny, dear Johnny,
Morning, noon and night,
I think of you marching,
Left, right, left and right.

3. I'm counting the minutes,
The hours and the days,
Oh Lord, stop the cruel war,
For this my heart prays.

4. The cruel war is raging,
Johnny has to fight,
But I'll be there with him,
From morning till night.

GUANTANAMERA

Cuban Song

Moderately

DS 𝄋 to Fine

JAMAICA FAREWELL

Brightly

Jamaican Song

⌢ This sign means to hold note longer.

IN THE EVENING BY THE MOONLIGHT

JAMES A. BLAND

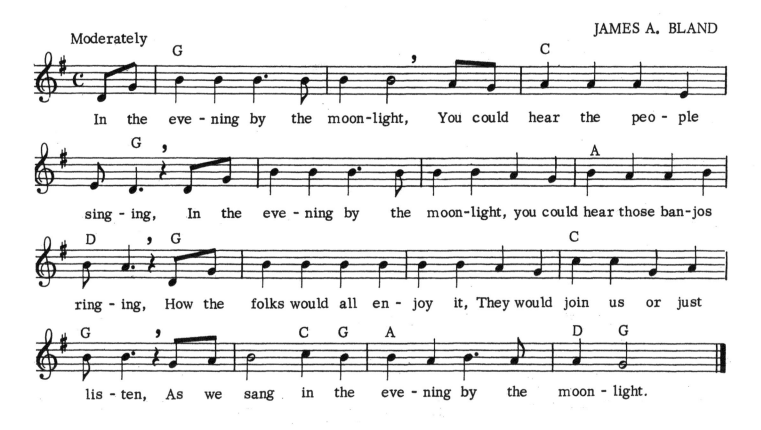

In the eve - ning by the moon-light, You could hear the peo - ple sing - ing, In the eve - ning by the moon-light, you could hear those ban-jos ring - ing, How the folks would all en - joy it, They would join us or just lis - ten, As we sang in the eve - ning by the moon - light.

SWEET AND LOW

JOSEPH BARNBY

Sweet and low, Sweet and low, Wind of the west-ern sea,____ Low, low, breathe and blow, Wind of the west - ern sea. ____ O - ver the roll - ing wa - ters go, Come from the dy - ing moon - and blow, Blow him a - gain to me, ____ While my lit - tle one, while my pret - ty one sleeps._____

THE ROSE OF TRALEE

Words by
C. MORDAUNT SPENCER

Music by
CHARLES W. GLOVER

Moderate waltz

I'LL TAKE YOU HOME AGAIN, KATHLEEN

THOMAS WESTENDORF

Moderately

I'll take you home a - gain, Kath - leen, A - cross the o - cean wild and

wide, To where your heart has ev - er been, Since

first you were my bon - ny bride. The ros - es all have left your

cheek, I've watched them fade a - way and die, Your

voice is sad when - e'er you speak, And tears be - dim your lov - ing

eyes. Oh I will take you back, Kath - leen, To

where your heart will feel no pain, And when the fields are fresh and

green, I will take you to your home a - gain.

LOCH LOMOND

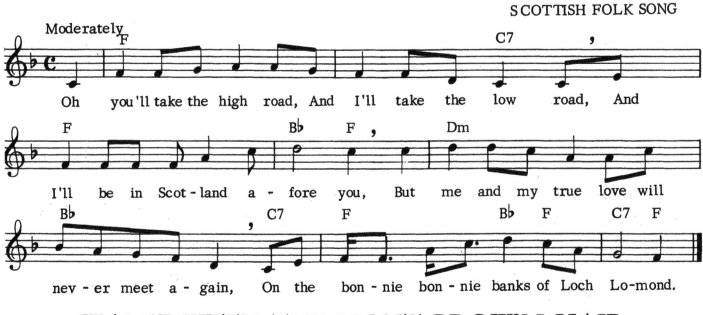

SCOTTISH FOLK SONG

Moderately

Oh you'll take the high road, And I'll take the low road, And I'll be in Scot-land a - fore you, But me and my true love will nev - er meet a - gain, On the bon - nie bon - nie banks of Loch Lo-mond.

JEANIE WITH THE LIGHT BROWN HAIR

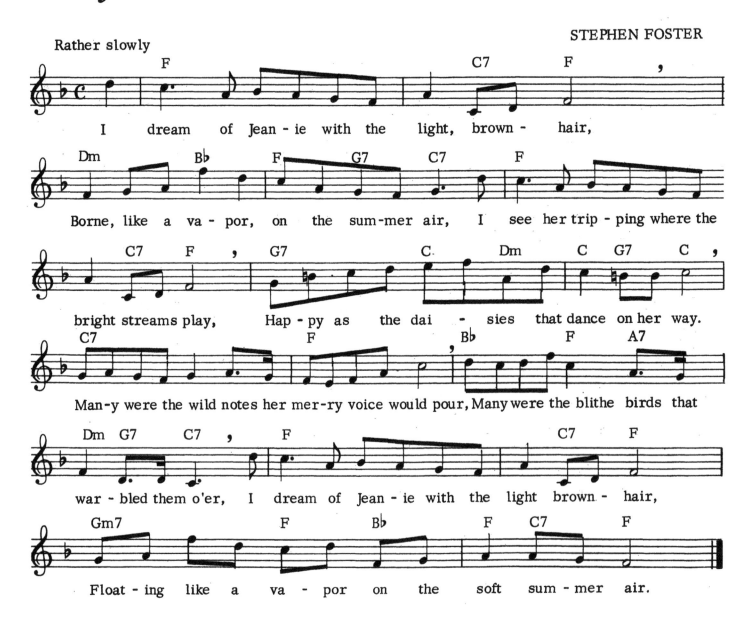

STEPHEN FOSTER

Rather slowly

I dream of Jean - ie with the light, brown - hair, Borne, like a va - por, on the sum-mer air, I see her trip - ping where the bright streams play, Hap - py as the dai - sies that dance on her way. Man-y were the wild notes her mer-ry voice would pour, Many were the blithe birds that war - bled them o'er, I dream of Jean - ie with the light brown - hair, Float - ing like a va - por on the soft sum - mer air.

THE OLD KENTUCKY HOME

STEPHEN FOSTER

OLD DOG TRAY

STEPHEN FOSTER

GIVE MY REGARDS TO BROADWAY

GEORGE M. COHAN

MARY'S A GRAND OLD NAME

GEORGE M. COHAN

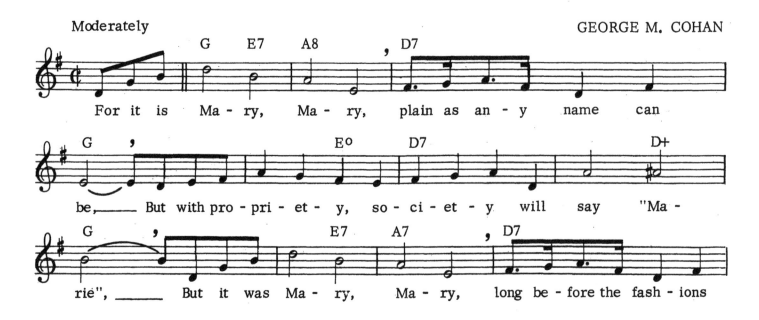

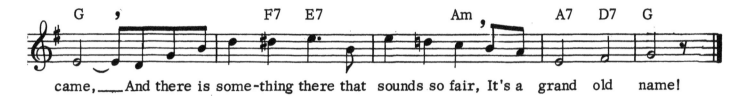

came,____ And there is some-thing there that sounds so fair, It's a grand old name!

THE YANKEE DOODLE BOY

Spirited march tempo

GEORGE M. COHAN

I'm a Yan - kee Doo - dle dan - dy, A

Yan - kee Doo - dle, do or die,____ A

real live neph - ew of my Un - cle Sam,

Born on the Fourth of Ju - ly.____ I've

got a Yan - kee Doo - dle sweet - heart,

She's my Yan - kee Doo - dle joy.____

Yan - kee Doo - dle came to Lon - don just to ride the po - nies,

I am a Yan - kee Doo - dle boy.____

84

With spirit

THOMAS A. BECKET

O. Co - lum-bia, the gem of the o - cean, The home of the brave - and the free, - The

shrine of each pa-triot's de -vo -tion, A world - of-fers hom - age to thee. Thy -

man-dates make he - roes as - sem-ble, When Li-ber-ty's form - stands in view, Thy -

ban-ners make tyr -an-ny trem-ble, When - borne - by the red, white and blue,___

CHORUS

When - borne by the red, white and blue, When - borne by the red, white and blue, Thy -

ban-ners make tyr - an - ny trem-ble, When - borne - by the red, white and blue.___

HAIL TO THE CHIEF

Words by
Albert Gamse
Slow march tempo

Music by
JAMES SANDERSON

Hail to the Chief we have chos - en for the na - tion, Hail to the

Chief! We sa - lute him, one and all. Hail to the Chief, as we

pledge co - op - er - a - tion - In proud ful - fill - ment of a great, no - ble

call. Yours is the aim to make this grand coun - try grand - er,

This you will do, That's our strong, firm be - lief. Hail to the one we se -

lect - ed as com - mand - er, Hail to the Pres - i - dent! Hail to the Chief!

BLACK IS THE COLOR OF
MY TRUE LOVE'S HAIR

Slowly

Folk Song

Dm   Gm   Dm   C   Dm

Black is the col-or of my true love's__ hair, Her

Gm   Bb   A

lips _____ are like the rose so fair, ____ And the

Gm   Bb   A

charm of her face and the soft-ness of her

Dm   Bb   A   D

hands, I love _____ the ground on which she stands. _____

THE BIG ROCK CANDY MOUNTAIN

Lively

C   G7   Folk Song

C   G7   C   G7

C   G7   C   G7

C   G7

C   C   C7   F

C   G7   C   G7   C

WHEN JOHNNY COMES MARCHING HOME

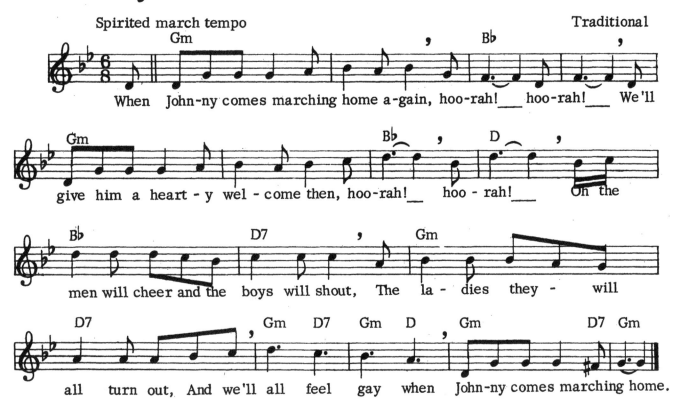

THE CRAWDAD SONG

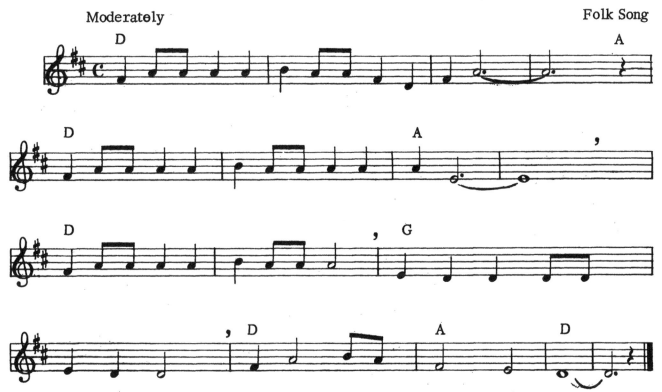

COME BACK TO SORRENTO

Slowly

ERNESTO DE CURTIS

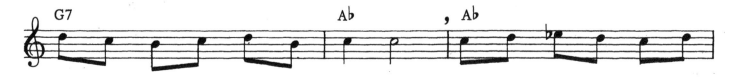

O SOLE MIO

Moderately

EDUARDO DI CAPUA

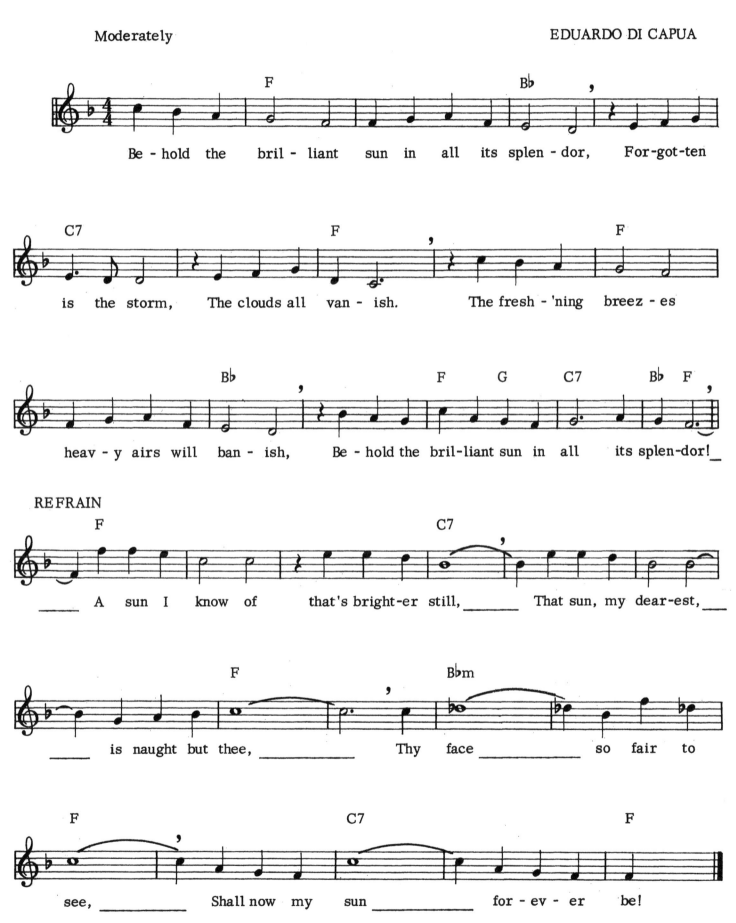

KASHMIRI SONG
(PALE HANDS I LOVED)

Words by
LAURENCE HOPE

Music by
AMY W. FINDEN

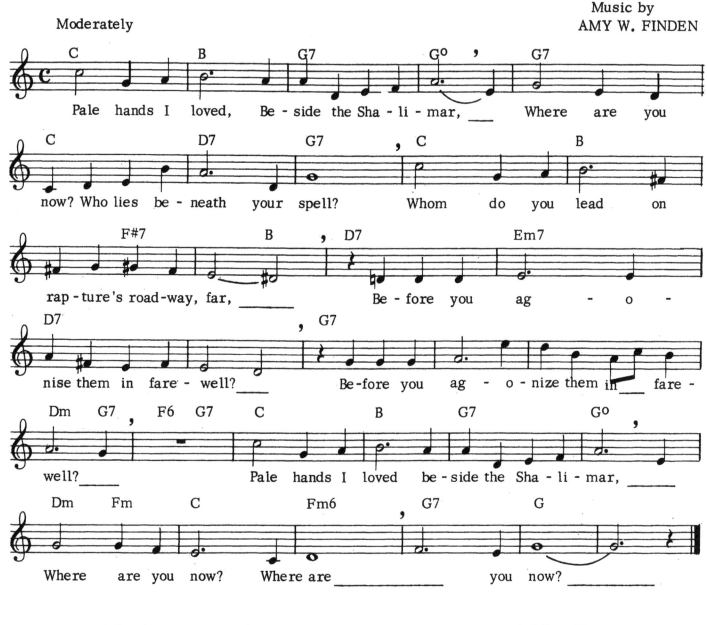

Pale hands I loved, Be - side the Sha - li - mar, ___ Where are you now? Who lies be - neath your spell? Whom do you lead on rap - ture's road - way, far, _____ Be - fore you ag - o - nise them in fare - well?___ Be - fore you ag - o - nize them in___ fare - well?_____ Pale hands I loved be - side the Sha - li - mar, ____ Where are you now? Where are _____ you now? _____

THE SWEETEST STORY EVER TOLD

Rather slowly

R. M. STULTS

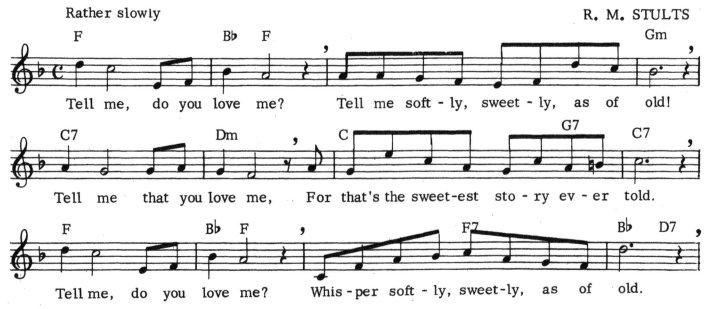

Tell me, do you love me? Tell me soft - ly, sweet - ly, as of old! Tell me that you love me, For that's the sweet - est sto - ry ev - er told. Tell me, do you love me? Whis - per soft - ly, sweet - ly, as of old.

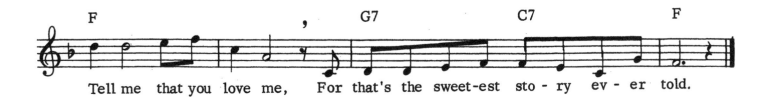

Tell me that you love me, For that's the sweet-est sto - ry ev - er told.

FASCINATION

F. D. MARCHETTI

Oh! the fas - ci - na - tion of you!

Oh! it's fas - ci - nat - ing to have you so near!

I re - mem - ber still what a won - drous thrill

Came in - to my heart, when I met you, my dear one!

Ev - 'ry day was lone - ly and blue,

Then you came a - long like a song from a - bove,

Sud - den - ly I felt more than just fas - ci - na - tion,

Sud - den - ly I fell in love!

A DREAM

Moderate waltz

CHARLES B. CORY

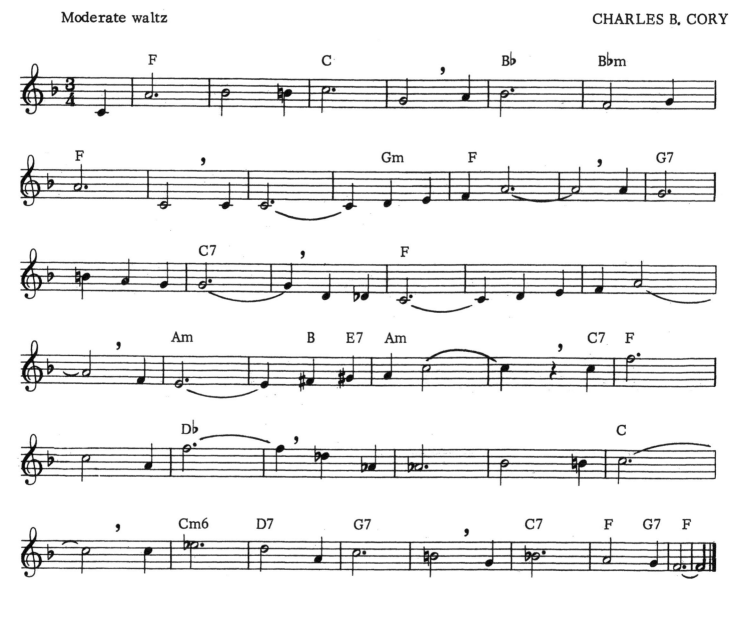

MELODY OF LOVE

Moderate waltz

H. ENGELMANN

SKATERS' WALTZ

Moderate waltz

EMIL WALDTEUFEL

Fine

DS 𝄋 al Fine

WHEN YOU WERE SWEET SIXTEEN

Slowly

JAMES THORNTON

I love you as I nev-er loved be-fore, _____ Since

first I met you on the vil-lage green. _____ Come to me or my

dream of love is o'er, _____ I love you as I loved you, ___

_____ When you were sweet, _____ when you were sweet six - teen. _____

HELLO! MA BABY

Words by
JOSEPH HOWARD

Music by
IDA EMERSON

Hel - lo! ma ba - by, Hel-lo! ma hon - ey, Hel - lo! ma rag - time

gal. Send me a kiss by wire, Ba - by, ma heart's on

fire! If you re - fuse me, hon - ey, you'll lose me, Then you'll be left a -

lone, Oh! ba - by, tel - e - phone, and tell me I'm your

own, Hel-lo! Hel - lo! Hel - lo there! own. _____

DEAR OLD GIRL

Words by
RICHARD BUCK

Music by
THEODORE MORSE

MY GAL SAL

Moderate waltz

PAUL DRESSER

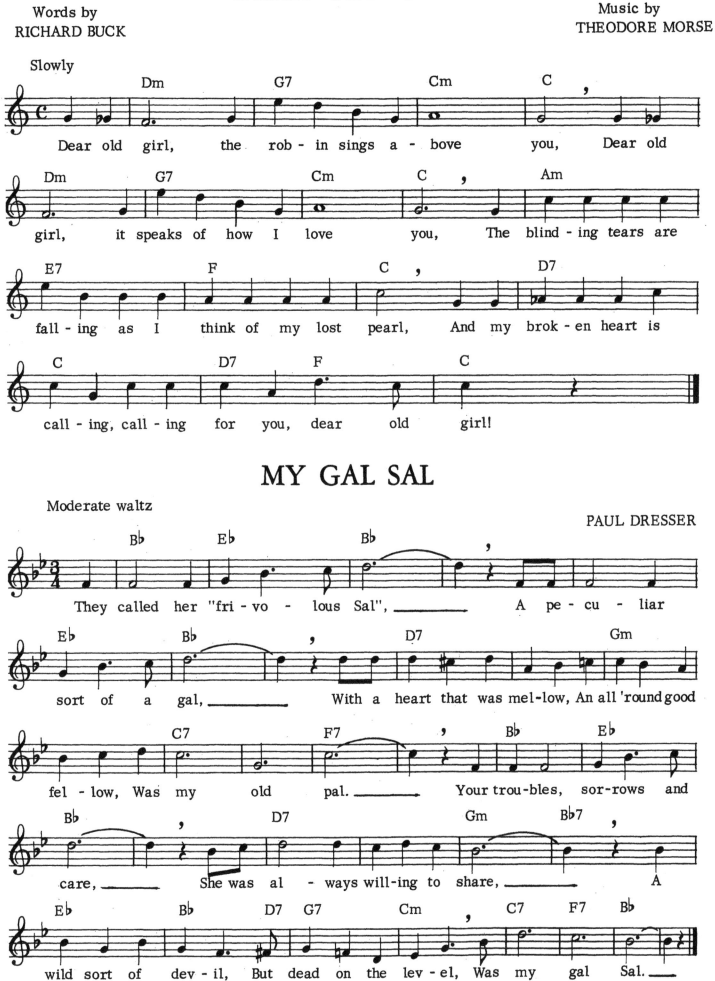

THE ROSARY

Words by
ROBERT ROGERS

Music by
ETHELBERT NEVIN

Slowly

The hours I spent with thee, dear heart, _____ Are as a string of pearls to me. _____ I count them o - ver ev - 'ry one a - part, My ro - sa - ry, my ro - sa - ry! Each hour a pearl, each pearl a pray'r, _____ To still a heart in ab - sence wrung, _____ I tell each bead un - to the end, And there a cross is hung! Oh mem - o - ries that bless and burn! _____ Oh bar - ren gain and bit - ter loss! _____ I kiss each bead and strive at last to learn, To kiss the cross, sweet - heart! To kiss the cross. _____

JESU, JOY OF MAN'S DESIRING

Note. - A simplified form of reading: Disregard triplets and play in 3/8 time, consider each group of three 8th notes as a separate measure. In that case, the quarter notes and rests will be dotted and final measure will consist of three dotted quarter notes.

JOHANN SEBASTIAN BACH
(From Cantata No. 147)

Moderately and smoothly

NOTE. - In the DUETS and TRIOS that follow, the top line may be played SOLO.

DUET SELECTIONS

BLOW THE MAN DOWN

Moderate waltz

Folk Song

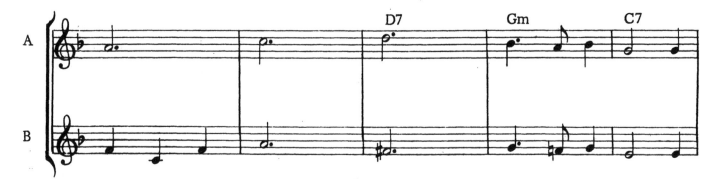

MARY ANN

West Indian Song

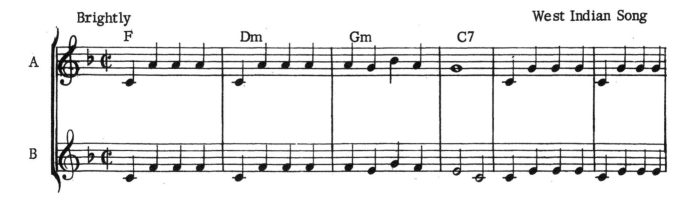

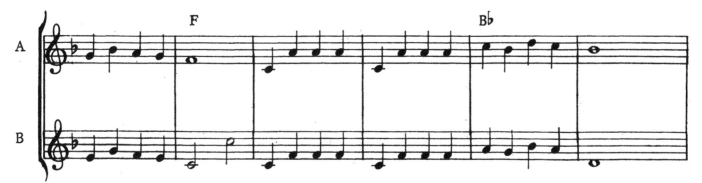

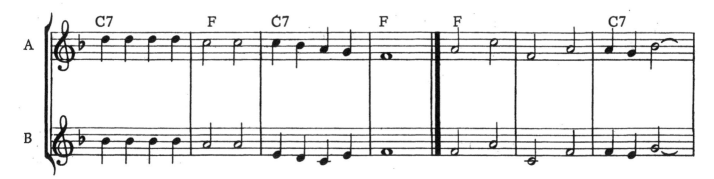

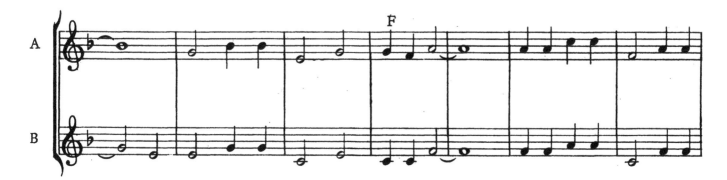

LONDONDERRY AIR

Slowly

IRISH MELODY

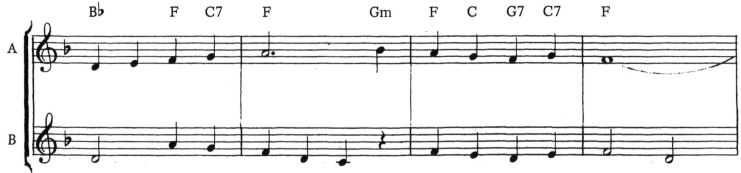

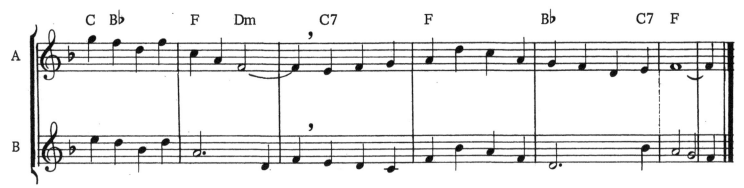

THE KERRY DANCE

J. L. MOLLOY

ALLEGRETTO

WOLFGANG AMADEUS MOZART

Moderately fast

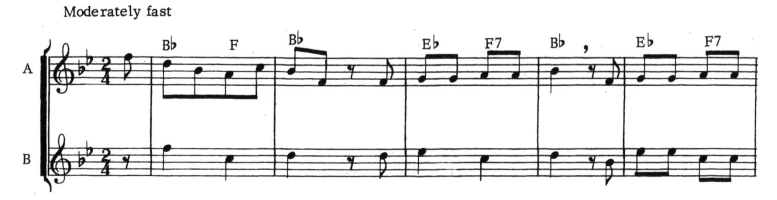

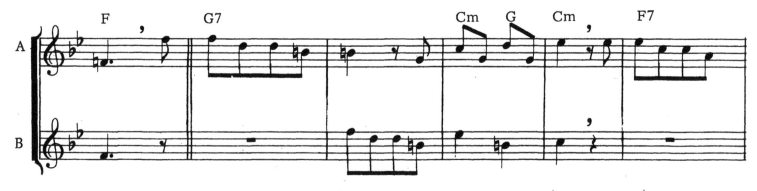

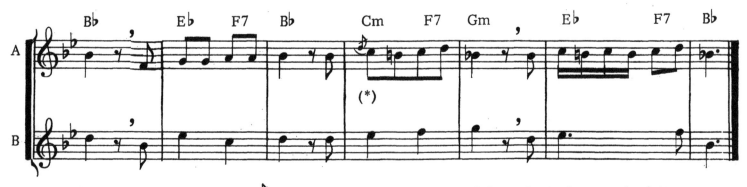

* This is a "grace note: ♪ It partakes of the time of the principal note, the latter taking the accent.

COME TO THE SEA

(Vieni Sul Mar)

Moderate waltz

Italian melody

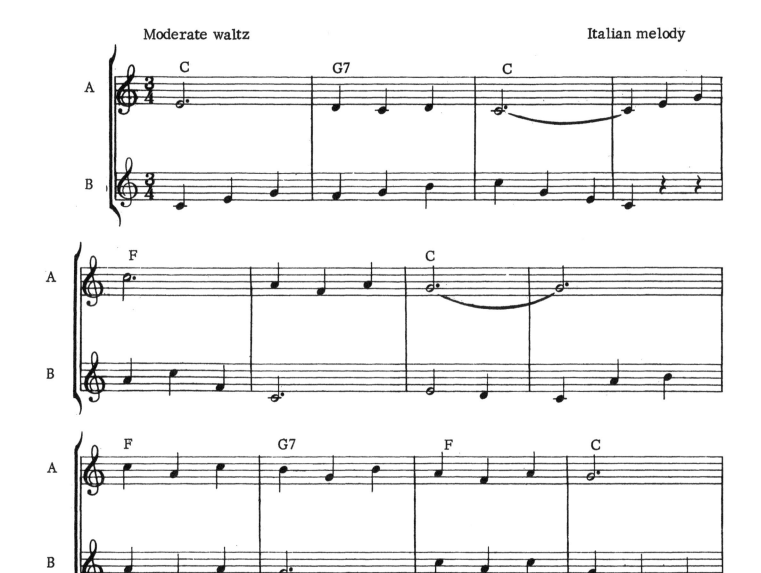

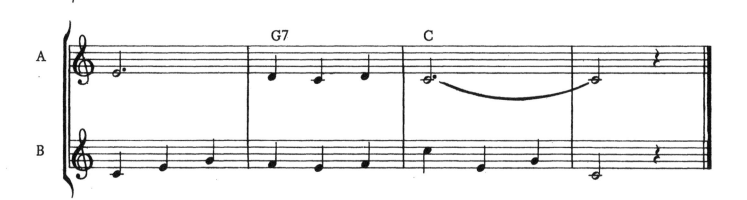

NORWEGIAN SONG

(Translated from Norwegian)

(TRUE LOVE)

Slowly

EDVARD GRIEG

True love is the same when the win-try breez-es blow, As when summer flowers grow

_____ True love remains the same in the au-tumn or the spring, And of

such a love I sing,_____ Of such a love I sing, This, my song, brings to you a

mes-sage from a-bove: With all my heart I pledge love for you, on-ly you, I

pledge to you true love! (Instrumental interlude)

(Fine)

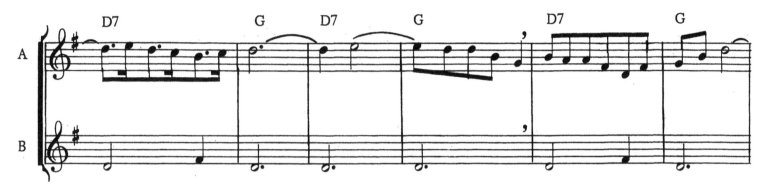

HUNGARIAN DANCE No. 5

JOHANNES BRAHMS

Fast, with spirit

LA GOLONDRINA
(THE SWALLOW)

Mexican waltz
Moderately

NARCISO SERRADELL

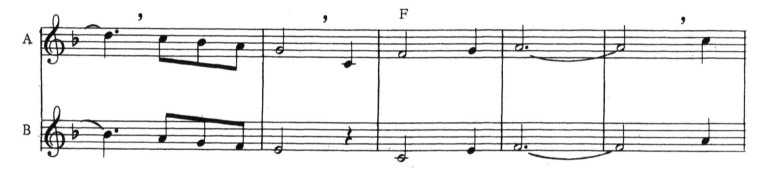

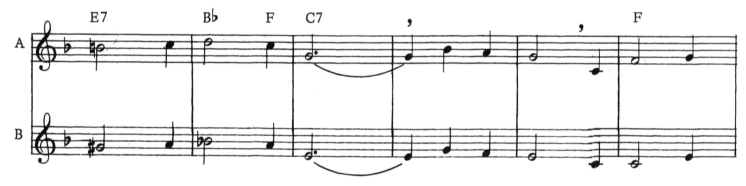

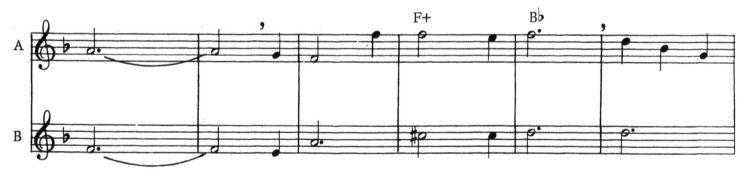

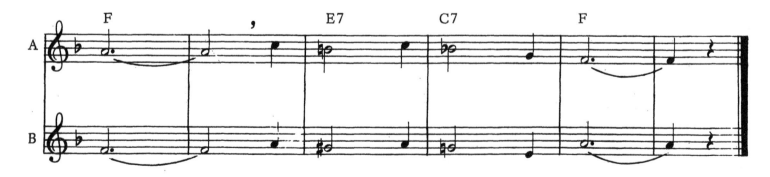

THE YELLOW ROSE OF TEXAS

With spirit

TEXAN FOLK SONG

She's the sweet-est lit - tle la - dy, A fel - low ev - er knew, Her

eyes are bright as dia - monds, They spark-le in the dew. You'll

see a lot of dam - sels as love - ly as can be, But the

yel - low Rose of Tex - as is the on - ly girl for me.

MEN OF HARLACH

Spirited march tempo

WELSH FOLK MELODY

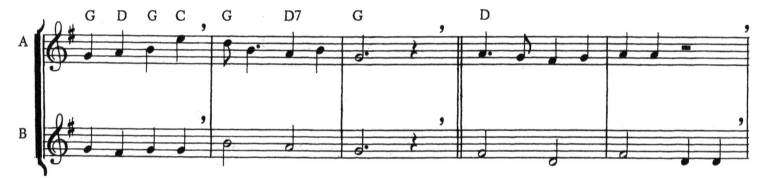

CARELESS LOVE

Moderately

FOLK SONG

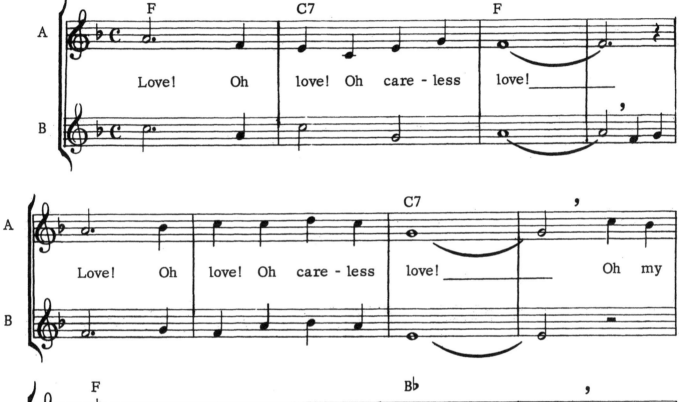

Love! Oh love! Oh care - less love!

Love! Oh love! Oh care - less love! Oh my

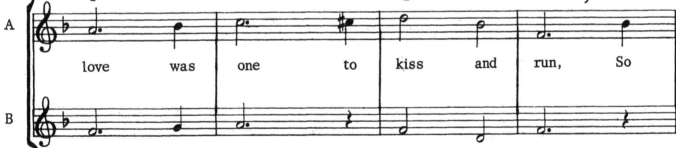

love was one to kiss and run, So

look what care - less love has done.

GAVOTTE

Moderately fast

FRANCOIS GOSSEC

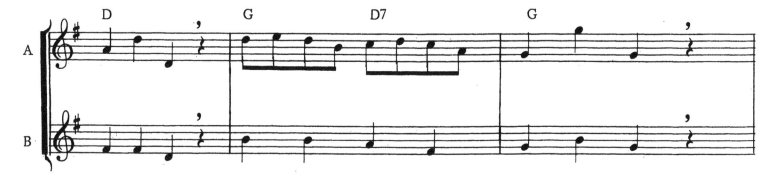

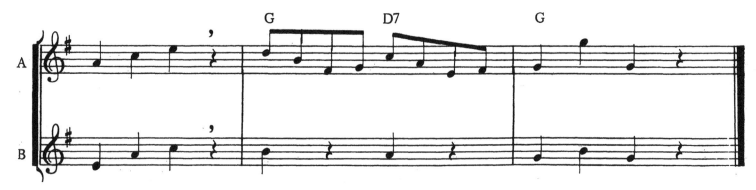

HUMORESQUE

ANTON DVORAK

Rather slowly

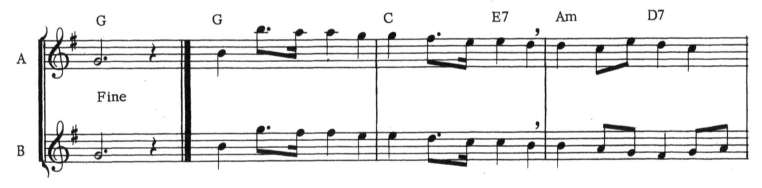

DS 𝄋 al Fine

LA PALOMA

(THE DOVE)

Moderately fast

SEBASTIAN YRADIER

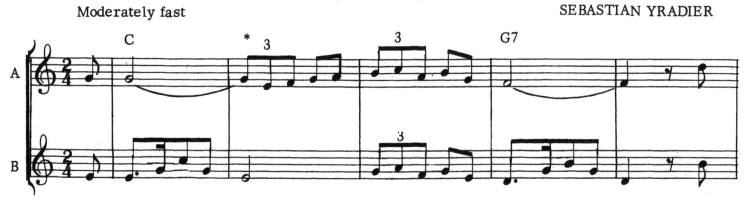

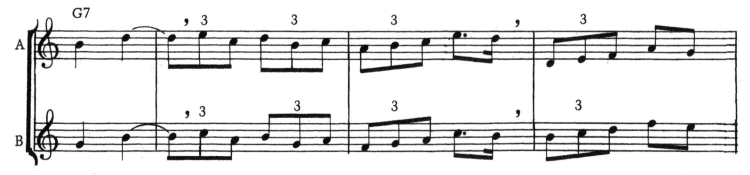

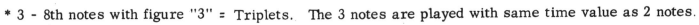

* 3 - 8th notes with figure "3" = Triplets.   The 3 notes are played with same time value as 2 notes.

DUTCH WALTZ

Bright waltz tempo

FOLK MELODY

CIELITO LINDO
(BEAUTIFUL HEAVEN)

Moderate waltz tempo

MEXICAN FOLK SONG

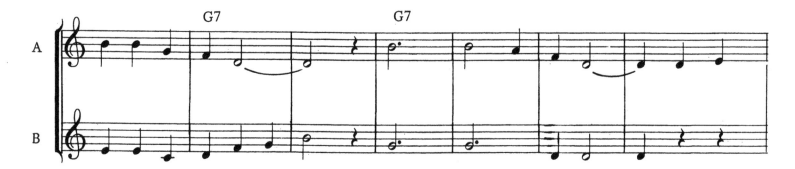

ANNIVERSARY WALTZ

Moderately

JAN IVANOVICI

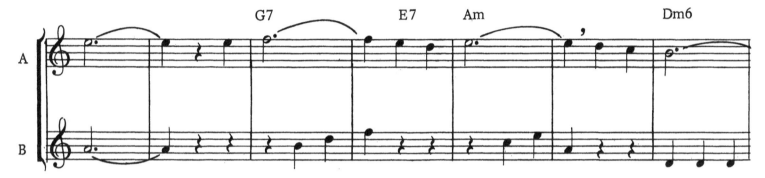

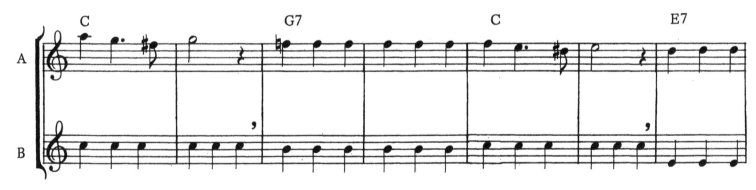

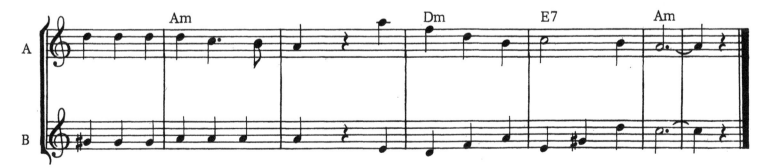

TRIO SELECTIONS

ACH! DU LIEBER AUGUSTIN

Bright waltz tempo

GERMAN FOLK SONG

COUNTRY DANCE

Moderately

FRANZ SCHUBERT

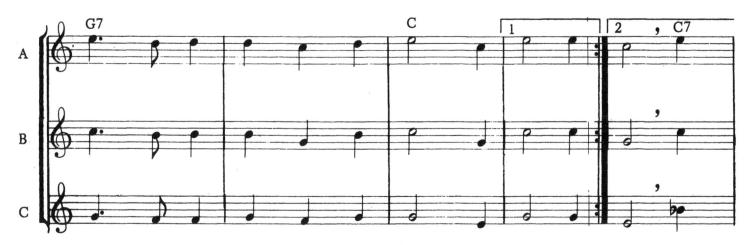

MERRY WIDOW WALTZ

FRANZ LEHAR

Moderately

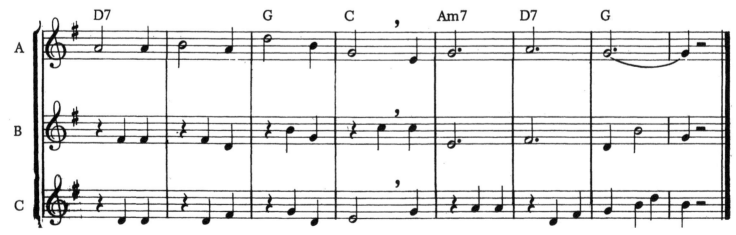

MARCHE MILITAIRE

Bright march tempo

FRANZ SCHUBERT

THE POEM

Slow waltz

ZDENKO FIBICH

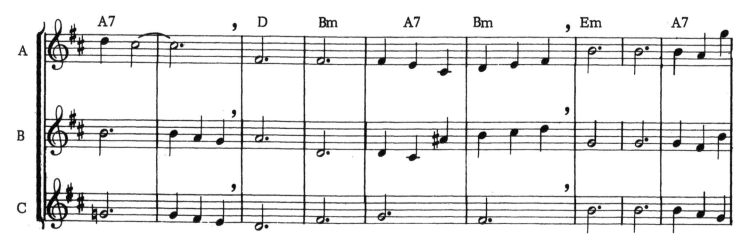

ROSES FROM THE SOUTH

Moderate waltz tempo

JOHANN STRAUSS

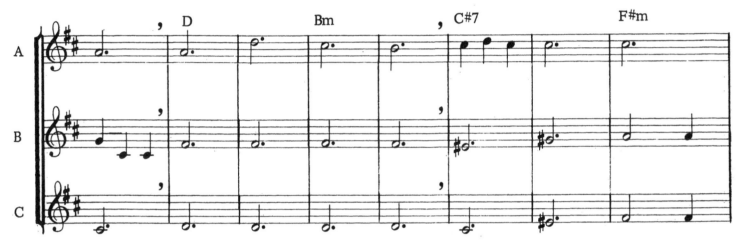

HABANERA
(FROM "CARMEN")

GEORGES BIZET

123

IN THE MERRY MONTH OF MAY

FELIX MENDELSSOHN

COME BACK TO ERIN

DARK EYES

Rather slowly

Russian Song

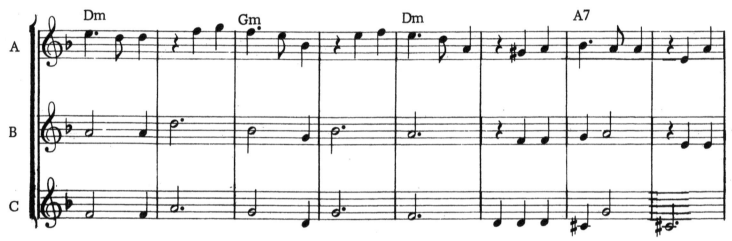

In The Shade Of The Old Apple Tree

Slow waltz tempo

WILLIAMS-VAN ALSTYNE

In the shade of the old ap - ple tree, ___ Where the

love in your eyes I could see, ___ When the

voice that I heard, Like the song of the bird, Seemed to

whis - per sweet mu - sic to me. ___ I could